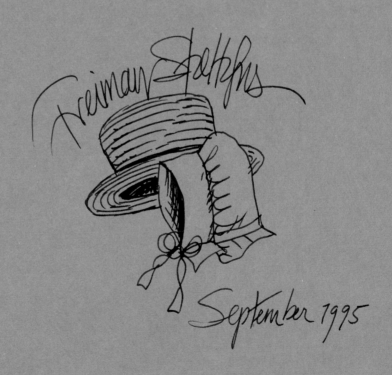

Freiman Stoltzfus

September 1995

A IS FOR AMISH

First Printing March, 1993.
Second Printing August, 1994.

A IS FOR AMISH

By Kim Gehman Knisely
Illustrated By Freiman Stoltzfus

This book is dedicated to my
children Amanda and Jeremy
who have been my greatest gift
and source of inspiration.
I also thank my family for all
of their invaluable guidance
and unwavering support.

KGK

The Artist wishes to thank his
family for their support and his
Heavenly Father for the gift of
creativity.

FFS

The Amish have lived in Pennsylvania since the early 1700's. For over two hundred years the way they live has undergone little change. Lancaster County, Pennsylvania became the settling ground for the Amish due, in part, to the rich, fertile land on which they built their farms. Most Amish are farmers who have chosen to live in harmony with the land and to live a conservative lifestyle. Their homes do not have electricity, there are no televisions, radios or telephones. The Amish strive to maintain a quiet, simple way of living.

Have you seen the horses and buggies on the highway? Did you know that Amish children attend private school? What kind of toys do Amish children play with? How many letters of the alphabet can you recognize? This book will start you on your way to learning some interesting facts about the Amish, the area where they live, and the alphabet too.

Aa

Amish

The Amish are a quiet, gentle group of Christian people who have chosen to live differently from most persons throughout the World.

Bb

Buggy

The buggy is the Amish person's means of transportation. The Amish do not drive cars, they are considered too worldly.

Cc

Covered Bridge

Many covered bridges cross streams in Lancaster County adding to the scenic beauty of the area.

Dd

Doll

This doll would be homemade, without a face, and is typical of what a young Amish girl would play with. Amish dolls appear faceless based on religious beliefs, one of which is that engraved images are prohibited. It is also for this reason that Amish people prefer not to be photographed.

Ee

Elder

The elders of the Amish community are respected for their long years of hard work and vast knowledge. Amish people do not place their aging relatives in nursing homes, they believe it is their duty to care for them.

Ff

Farm and Field

Most Amish are farmers who work the fields with mules or horses. Tractors are not used in the fields of an Amish farmer.

Gg
Garden

The garden is the wife's responsibility. An Amish wife raises many fruits and vegetables and grows a great variety of flowers.

Hh

Horse

Horses are owned by an Amish family for pulling the buggy. Larger horses are also used for work in the fields because Amish farmers do not use tractors.

Ii

Ice
Skating

A popular winter
sport for Amish
youth, ice skating
provides a social time
for exercise and fun.

Jj

Jump
Rope

The jump rope is a
favorite plaything on
a bright sunny day.
Amish children do
not own many store
bought toys.

Kk

Kerosene Lantern

A kerosene lantern is used to read the Bible or sew by at nighttime. Amish do not use electricity in their homes.

Ll

Lunch Pail

Amish children carry their lunch to school each day.
Noontime recess is filled with games and fun.

Mm

Mother

The primary role of an Amish mother is to provide the care and love necessary for her children to grow and learn the Amish ways. Her day is filled doing housework, sewing clothes, maintaining the garden and occasionally helping in the fields.

Nn

Neighbor

An Amish family's closest neighbor may live a mile or more away. Amish parents prefer to keep their children away from outside influences so Amish children most often play with their brothers and sisters or other Amish neighbors.

Oo

Open Carriage

Young Amish men drive the open carriage while they are courting. A conventional closed carriage will be purchased following the wedding. Once married the Amish man allows his beard to grow.

Pp

Prayer Cap

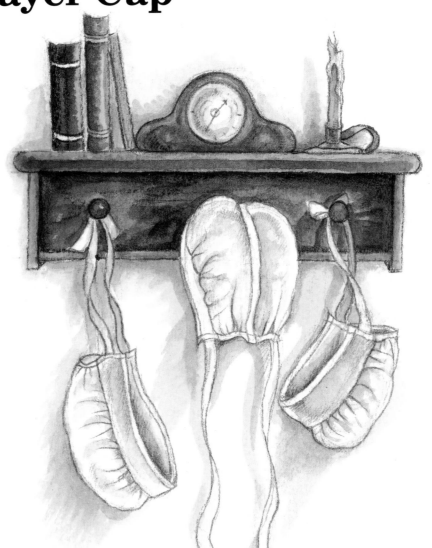

The prayer cap or head covering is one of the most symbolic garments of the Amish women. This covering is worn in obedience to the Bible's command that the head shall always be covered.

Qq

Quilt

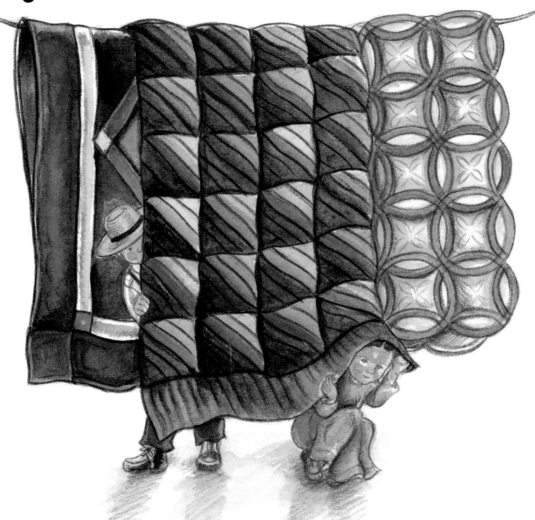

Beautiful quilts in many different patterns are created by Amish women. Quilting bees are a major social function for the women in the Amish community.

Rr

Roadside Market

To supplement the family income some Amish women will sell the produce from their garden at small markets beside their homes. These small home markets are commonly referred to as roadside stands.

Ss

School

Amish children attend private school through the eighth grade. All students are taught by one teacher in a one room school house.

Tt

Teacher

The teacher for an Amish school is selected from within the Amish community, she is usually unmarried with no more than an eighth grade education. Her duty is to teach her students the basics of reading, writing and arithmetic.

Uu

Umbrella

Store-bought items, such
as the umbrella, are both
useful and necessary.

Vv

Vest

An Amish man is easily identified by his style of dress. A black vest, felt or straw hat and plain colored shirt are traditionally worn.

Ww

Windmill

The windmill is used by the Amish to pump water to their homes.

Xx

Sewing, done by hand, is taught to girls at an early age. The x forms one of the first stitches that a young Amish girl learns.

Yy

Yoke

A yoke is placed around the neck of horses or mules and connects them to the plow when they are working in the fields.

Zz

Zipper

Amish people do not use zippers on their clothes.
Hooks and eyes or straight pins are used because the
Amish believe zippers are too modern.

The End

This book has been manufactured in Lancaster County, Pennsylvania.

Printed by Science Press, 300 West Chestnut Street, Ephrata, PA